AI

Artificial Intelligence Fundamentals, AI-900, and Manufacturing

STEM ®

AI

ARTIFICIAL Intelligence Fundamentals,

AI-900, and Manufacturing

Omar Silva-Fulchi, PMP, P.Eng.

Original Title: AI

ISBN: 9798396985520

First Edition, July 2023

Independently Published

DEDICATION I

I dedicated this book to the loving memory of my father, Omar Miguel, and my mother, Teresa de Jesus, who influenced my childhood.

In memory of my dear wife Blankita, with whom we had two amazing children, Omar, and Karen.

DEDICATION II

I dedicated this book to my cherished children, Omar & Yara, and Karen & Ali, who helped me with their valuable visions and work at Robo-Geek, and my dear grandchildren: Andrea, AnnaSophia, Omar Fernando, and Alexandra.

This book is dedicated to my dear relatives and my beloved wife, Liz, who supported me in developing this book. Also, to her children Jorge & Ying, Jenny & Andy, Ron & Judy, and grandchildren Ava, Kaelyn, Joshua, Lucas, Ethan, Caleb, Micah, and Josh.

CONTACT LINKS

Omar Silva-Fulchi

Facebook

Facebook

YouTube Channel

YouTube

Email

info@robo-geek.ca

Omar Silva-Fulchi   AI   <u>info@robo-geek.ca</u>

TABLE OF CONTENTS

INTRODUCTION

Miraflores, a district In Lima, Peru, has built a magnificent boulevard along the coast where visitors can bike, jog, walk, or spend gorgeous moments surrounded by breathtaking scenery. The district is home to over sixty-four species of trees, like Ficus, real poinciana, African tulip, eucalyptus, yellow bells, ash tree, jacaranda, and cedar. Every morning I would greet the workers on my way to the gym and couldn't help but compare their methods to those used in Canada. Street sweeping is manual labor in Peru, whereas Canada Municipalities use sweeper trucks. As our countries evolve, robots or machines replace manual labor tasks, taking jobs from the market.

In the 60s and 70s, America started outsourcing and offshoring textile industries and manufacturing to lower-cost countries.

Everyone is concerned about how AI, known as Artificial Intelligence, will affect our lives, jobs, and finances. This book introduces you to the AI fundamental principles and technologies in AI.

OpenAI released ChatGPT™-4 on March 14, 2023. GPT™-4 solves complex problems accurately and is creative. Moreover, it can compose songs and write screenplays. Additionally, it passed the SAT and Uniform Bar Exams with top percentiles.

All these accomplishments have scared people into thinking about their future and job stability.

This book introduces you to the fundamental principles of Artificial Intelligence (AI) and related technologies.

Part IV contains information about GPT (Generative Pre-trained Transformer) AI, what it is, and how it will affect our daily life, the economy, and jobs.

In Part II, Chapter IV, this book analyzes how AI applies innovative technologies in the Manufacturing Industry using Twin Digital Models to optimize costs and production. Microsoft®, Google®, IBM®, and Siemens® also use the Twin Digital Models to predict and resolve failures on intelligent factory production lines in manufacturing.

In Chapters I, III, V – IX, you can find material and exercises to learn about AI areas and prepare for the AI-900 Microsoft Azure AI fundamentals Exam.

On May 04, 2023, VP Kamala Harris met with the heads of Google, Microsoft, Antrophic, and OpenAI to discuss the risks in the development of AI.

Chapter X, this book provides an up-to-date summary of the latest developments in AI at the publishing date.

Omar Silva-Fulchi   AI   info@robo-geek.ca

Omar Silva-Fulchi   AI   info@robo-geek.ca

PART I

Omar Silva-Fulchi   AI   <u>info@robo-geek.ca</u>

Chapter I

Artificial Intelligence at Microsoft

What is Microsoft artificial intelligence?

Microsoft Artificial intelligence is a set of computer systems that can execute tasks that usually need a human being's brain. Speech recognition, decision-making, and vision recognition are characteristics of individuals that artificial intelligence has now.

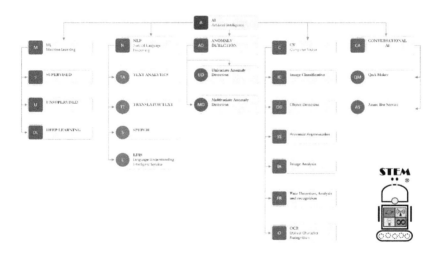

Artificial Intelligence
Machine Learning (ML)

Supervised Learning

Unsupervised learning

Deep Learning

ROBO-GEEK

MACHINE LEARNING

Machine learning (ML) is the method by which computers develop the ability to learn from data and make predictions based on the acquired knowledge.

Machine learning is a type of AI that lets computers adapt to new situations autonomously.

There are three types of systems in machine learning:

Supervised learning uses labeled data and requires less training.

Unsupervised learning helps classify unlabeled data by identifying relationships and associations with patterns.

Deep Learning Semi-supervised learning combines supervised learning with small, labeled data to categorize unsupervised unlabeled data sets.

Artificial Intelligence
Natural Language Processing (NLP)

Text Analytics

Translator Text

Speech

Luis

ROBO-GEEK

NATURAL LANGUAGE PROCESSING

Natural Language Processing (NLP) focuses on helping computers to develop the ability to speak with, hear and understand users.

Microsoft uses Microsoft Azure to build applications that support natural language.

NLP includes four services:

> **Text Analytics**: This service helps analyze text documents, extract key phrases, determine entities, provide sentiment analysis, and detect their language.

> **Translator Text**: This service translates texts in real time for 100+ languages.

> **Speech**: This service provides text-to-speech and speech-to-text resources to the users' apps. It can synthesize speech and translate live or recorded speech.

21

Language Understanding Intelligent Service (LUIS): This service allows your application to understand what a person wants in their own words.

ANOMALY DETECTION

Anomaly detection is a technique that uses AI to identify abnormal behavior in an established pattern. Anomaly is everything that diverges from an established baseline pattern.

Anomaly Detector is an AI service with a set of APIs; that allows you to monitor and detect anomalies in your time series data with little machine learning (ML) knowledge.

Univariate Anomaly Detection: This API detects anomalies in one variable, like profits and prices. ML selects the model automatically based on your data pattern.

Multivariate Detection: This API detects anomalies in multiple variables with correlations. ML selects the model from another complex system.

Artificial Intelligence
Computer Vision (CV)

Image Classification
Object Detection
Semantic Segmentation
Image Analysis
Face Detection, Analysis and recognition
OCR (Optical character recognition)

COMPUTER VISION (CV)

Computer Vision uses Machine Learning models trained for images and videos. There are six Computer Vision services:

Image classification: this service analyzes images and videos, detects objects and text, extracts descriptions, and creates tags.

Object detection: this service identifies objects and their boundaries within the image.

Semantic segmentation: this service identifies the pixels that belong to determined objects.

Image analysis: this service extracts information from the images, tags them, and creates a descriptive image summary.

Face detection, analysis, and recognition: this service detects, analyzes, and recognizes human faces.

23

Optical character recognition: this service detects and recognizes text in images and documents.

CONVERSATIONAL AI

Conversational AI has a set of tools to configure online chatbots. These chatbots are used in customer service to communicate with end-users using their natural languages.

Conversational AI employs ML and NLP to collect and analyze expressions, understand them, and then make persons' responses.

> **QnA Maker:** This service helps to create a knowledge base, a foundation for a conversation between humans and AI agents.

> **Azure Bot Service**: This service helps to create, publish, and manage Conversational AI agents or bots.

Chapter II

Artificial Intelligence at Google

Google launched AI Principles in 2018, they built and evaluated a governance process to align AI projects across Google with those Principles.

Google governance has three pillars:

- **AI Principles**, which serve as an ethical charter and inform Google policies.
- **Education and resources**, such as ethics training and technical tools to evaluate and monitor the usage of the Google AI Principles in all the products and services.
- **AI frameworks for risk assessment** of processes, ethics reviews, and management accountability. (Google-AI-01)

Google AI Principles

These are the Google AI Principles:

Be socially beneficial: Benefit people and society substantially exceed the foreseeable risks and downsides.

Avoid creating unfair bias: Avoiding unjust impacts on people, particularly those related tos ensetivecharacteristics such as race, ethnicity, gender, nationality, income, sexual orientation, and political or religious belief.

Be built and tested for safety: AI system design should be cautious and follow best practices in AI safety.

Be accountable to people: Provide opportunities for feedback, relevant explanations, and appeal.

Incorporate privacy design principles.

Uphold high standards of scientific excellence.

Google will not design AI in the following areas:

Technologies that cause or are likely to cause overall harm.

Weapons or other technologies that cause or directly facilitate injury to people.

Technologies that gather or use the information for surveillance, violating international norms.

Technologies that violate principles of international law and human rights.

(Google-AI-01)

Colab Notebooks

What is Colab?

Collaboratory, or "Colab" for short, is a data analysis tool that combines code, output, and descriptive text into one document (interactive notebook).

Google connects your Colab notebook to a free powerful machine in its Cloud.

Colab usage is through a Chrome browser that allows you to write and execute Python with these advantages:

No extra software configurations.

Free access to GPUs.

Easy sharing.

Google provides free Colab Notebooks in its Cloud. Google Colab uses the Jupyter format in its notebooks on your Google Drive. Its name extension is ipynb.

We have shared the Colab "Colab First Program" created by Robo-Geek. **(Robo-Geek 2023)**

The user can choose what kind of machine the Virtual Machine has. Just select it from the Menu -> Runtime -> Change runtime as shown in the image below:

Users can configure the Colab Notebook with TPU, GPU, or CPU.

TPU: Tensor Processing Unit is highly optimized for large batches and CNNs and has the highest training throughput.

. **Google Cloud TPU**:

TPU is the custom-designed machine learning ASIC that powers Google products like Translate, Photos, Search, Assistant, and Gmail.

Using TPUs and machine learning will accelerate your company's success.

Here are images of Cloud TPU, and Cloud TPU v3 Pod, from Google site **(-TPU 2017)**

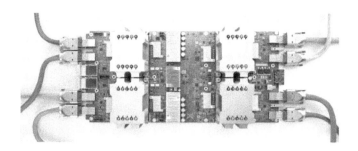

Google released Cloud TPU in May 2017 and its v4 in May 2022. This supercomputer contains 4,096 chips interconnected via proprietary optical circuit switches (OCS), which Google says are faster, cheaper, and utilize less power than InfiniBand. Google says its OCS technology is less than 5% of the TPU v4's system cost and power.

A "TPU pod" built with 64 second-generation TPUs delivers up to 11 5 petaflops of machine learning acceleration.

GPU: Graphics Processing Unit offers higher efficiency in manipulating image processing and computer graphics for their parallel structure.

Tesla uses its NVIDIA Tesla V100 Tensor Core with GPU in its Volta architecture. Below is an image of the NVIDIA Tesla V100 GPU.

CPU: Central Processing Unit achieves the highest FLOPS utilization for **RNN**s and supports the largest model because of its large memory capacity.

Below is an image of the Intel Server integrated with Microsoft Azure Stack HCI:

How to Create a Colab Notebook?

You need a Google account to create your Google Colab file; if you do not have an account, create one.

Now, click the "New" button at the top left corner of your Google Chrome.

Drive page, then click More ▷ Google Collaboratory.

The Operating System of the Colab Notebook is Ubuntu; its default CPU is a GPU with 14 GB of RAM and 100 GB of SD. Moreover, additional Python libraries are already in there.

Our sample Colab Notebook is the "Colab First program.". **(Robo-Geek 2023)**

31

The Colab notebook has Code cells, where you type your Python code, and Text cells, where you write the comments and notes about the cell you will run.

To know which libraries your notebook has, type and run the following command in one Code cell:

!pip freeze

Here is a snapshot of the list of libraries that the command freeze will display in the Google Colab notebook:

```
  1 !pip freeze
  2
scs==3.2.3
seaborn==0.12.2
Send2Trash==1.8.0
shapely==2.0.1
six==1.16.0
sklearn-pandas==2.2.0
smart-open==6.3.0
sniffio==1.3.0
snowballstemmer==2.2.0
sortedcontainers==2.4.0
soundfile==0.12.1
soupsieve==2.4.1
soxr==0.3.5
spacy==3.5.2
spacy-legacy==3.0.12
spacy-loggers==1.0.4
Sphinx==3.5.4
sphinxcontrib-applehelp==1.0.4
sphinxcontrib-devhelp==1.0.2
sphinxcontrib-htmlhelp==2.0.1
sphinxcontrib-jsmath==1.0.1
sphinxcontrib-qthelp==1.0.3
sphinxcontrib-serializinghtml==1.1.5
SQLAlchemy==2.0.10
```

Installing new libraries in the Colab Notebook is easy with the pip command.

Using Machine Learning with Google Colab

TensorFlow is an end-to-end open-source platform for machine learning. It has a complete and flexible set of tools, libraries, and online resources that lets programmers and developers analyze, develop, and deploy ML (Machine Learning) applications.

Google teams use them to train and learn with deep neural networks.

We found an interesting article at Laurence Moroney's link **(Moroney 2018)** on building a Convolutional Neural Network (CNN) for Rock, Paper, Scissors Project.

In the Summer of 2021, Varun and Azaan worked at Robo-Geek on this project., the detail of their findings is in the link **(Coop 2021)**. In this document, they explained their CNN projects and evaluated them using the free TensorFlow datasets available.

Inside this presentation, there is a slide that links to a "Machine Learning Explained" lecture by Laurence Moroney with Karmel Allison. The YouTube recording is at this link: **(I/O'19 2019).**

In the following lines, I explain the different blocks of code written in Python to create the Machine Learning (ML) model of "Rock, Paper, Scissors" using TensorFlow and Keras.

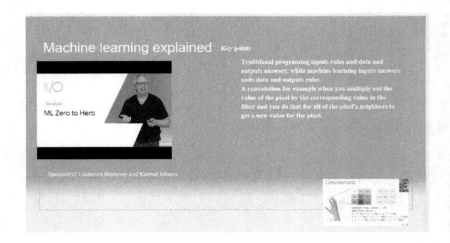

Machine Learning with TensorFlow

The installation of TensorFlow is complicated in Windows and versions other than 2.12 are not compatible. It is better to start with Google Colab to explore how Machine Learning works and how you can build the CNN (Convolutional Neural Network). Using the Notebook linked in the book will be a great start. **(Robo-Geek-CNN 2019)**

To optimize the learning speed of the CNN, the notebooks or servers require GPUs or TPUs; Colab notebook has access to a GPU or TPU.

Google provides free access to the Colab Notebooks but with limited hardware, only one GPU or TPU.

The libraries that we need to build the CNN are:

```
1 import tensorflow as tf    # importing Tensorflow library as tf
2 import tensorflow_datasets as tfds
3 import matplotlib.pyplot as plt
4 import numpy as np    # importing numpy library as np
5 import platform
6 import datetime
7 import os
8 import math
9 import random
```

To see the available TensorFlow datasets, just run the following:

```
1 # See available datasets
2 tfds.list_builders()
```

There are datasets on 3d, Abstractive text summarization, Anomaly detection, Audio, Biology, Common sense reasoning, computer science, D4rl, Density estimation, Dialogue, Fine-grained image classification, graph, image, image clustering, image generation, object detection, language modeling, and other categories.

Each dataset in TensorFlow contains the necessary logic to download the dataset and create an input pipeline.

For downloading the "rock paper scissors" dataset, use the command " (Coop 2021)DATASET_name = "rock_paper_scissors_" with its parameters as shown below:

```
1 DATASET_NAME = 'rock_paper_scissors'
2
3 (dataset_train_raw, dataset_test_raw), dataset_info = tfds.load(
4     name=DATASET_NAME,
5     data_dir='tmp',
6     with_info=True,
7     as_supervised=True,
8     split=[tfds.Split.TRAIN, tfds.Split.TEST],
9 )
```

Downloading and preparing dataset 219.53 MiB (download: 219.53 MiB, generated: Unknown size, total: 219.53 MiB) to tmp/rock_paper_scissors/3.0.0
Dl Completed... 100%   2/2 [00:02<00:00, 1.51s/ url]
Dl Size... 100%   219/219 [00:02<00:00, 81.78 MiB/s]
Dataset rock_paper_scissors downloaded and prepared to tmp/rock_paper_scissors/3.0.0. Subsequent calls will reuse this data.

CNN requires two datasets, the dataset_train_raw and the data_set_test_raw. The system uses the first one to train the CNN and the second to evaluate the parameters of the trained CNN.

If we use the command **"dataset_info,"** we can learn the different parameters that the dataset has.

```
1 dataset_info
```

```
tfds.core.DatasetInfo(
    name='rock_paper_scissors',
    full_name='rock_paper_scissors/3.0.0',
    description="""
    Images of hands playing rock, paper, scissor game.
    """,
    homepage='http://laurencemoroney.com/rock-paper-scissors-dataset',
    data_path=PosixGPath('/tmp/tmp3mt6x2iotfds'),
    file_format=tfrecord,
    download_size=219.53 MiB,
    dataset_size=219.23 MiB,
    features=FeaturesDict({
        'image': Image(shape=(300, 300, 3), dtype=uint8),
        'label': ClassLabel(shape=(), dtype=int64, num_classes=3),
    }),
    supervised_keys=('image', 'label'),
    disable_shuffling=False,
    splits={
        'test': <SplitInfo num_examples=372, num_shards=1>,
        'train': <SplitInfo num_examples=2520, num_shards=2>,
    },
    citation="""@ONLINE {rps,
    author = "Laurence Moroney",
    title = "Rock, Paper, Scissors Dataset",
    month = "feb",
    year = "2019",
    url = "http://laurencemoroney.com/rock-paper-scissors-dataset"
    }""",
)
```

The information you can extract from here is all we need to configure your CNN; in this case, we have the following:

name='rock_paper_scissors'

homepage='http://laurencemoroney.com/rock-paper-scissors-dataset'

download size=219.53 MiB, dataset size=219.23 MiB, image shape= (300, 300, 3), data type=uint8

label shape= data type=int64, number of classes=3

supervised keys=image and label.

splits=

test <Split Info number of examples=372, number of shards=1>

train <Split Info number of examples=2520, number of shards=2>

author = "Laurence Moroney",

title = "Rock, Paper, Scissors Dataset",

month = "Feb", year = "2019"

url   =http://laurencemoroney.com/rock-paper-scissors-dataset

GETTING INFORMATION FOR THE DATASETS

```
[10]   1 NUM_TRAIN_EXAMPLES = dataset_info.splits['train'].num_examples
       2 NUM_TEST_EXAMPLES = dataset_info.splits['test'].num_examples
       3 NUM_CLASSES = dataset_info.features['label'].num_classes
       4
       5 print('Number of TRAIN examples:', NUM_TRAIN_EXAMPLES)
       6 print('Number of TEST examples:', NUM_TEST_EXAMPLES)
       7 print('Number of label classes:', NUM_CLASSES)

Number of TRAIN examples: 2520
Number of TEST examples: 372
Number of label classes: 3
```

It is essential to verify the quality and accuracy of the data used in CNN.

The program shrinks the original images dataset and converts their color components in the scale range (0-255) to NumPy (0-1.0).

Another way to generalize the model to broader examples is to augment the training data.

TensorFlow has tools to augment the original data by applying images flip, rotation, and adjusting the background colors.

The method augment data includes the instructions to apply different transformations to the data:

```
1 def augment_data(image, label):
2     image = augment_flip(image)
3     image = augment_color(image)
4     image = augment_rotation(image)
5     image = augment_zoom(image)
6     image = augment_inversion(image)
7     return image, label
```

```
[31] 1 dataset_train_augmented = dataset_train.map(augment_data)
```

```
1 # Explore augmented training dataset.
2 preview_dataset(dataset_train_augmented)
```

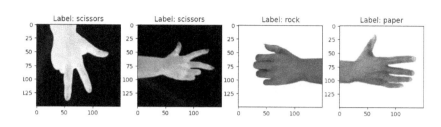

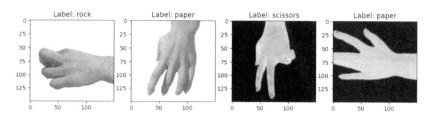

These images of rock, paper and scissors were obtained applying the augmented method. To the datasets

CREATING THE MODEL

+ Code   + Text

```python
1 model = tf.keras.models.Sequential()
2
3 # First convolution.
4 model.add(tf.keras.layers.Convolution2D(
5     input_shape=INPUT_IMG_SHAPE,
6     filters=64,
7     kernel_size=3,
8     activation=tf.keras.activations.relu
9 ))
10 model.add(tf.keras.layers.MaxPooling2D(
11     pool_size=(2, 2),
12     strides=(2, 2)
13 ))
14
15 # Second convolution.
16 model.add(tf.keras.layers.Convolution2D(
17     filters=64,
18     kernel_size=3,
19     activation=tf.keras.activations.relu
20 ))
21 model.add(tf.keras.layers.MaxPooling2D(
22     pool_size=(2, 2),
23     strides=(2, 2)
24 ))
25
26 # Third convolution.
27 model.add(tf.keras.layers.Convolution2D(
28     filters=128,
29     kernel_size=3,
30     activation=tf.keras.activations.relu
31 ))
32 model.add(tf.keras.layers.MaxPooling2D(
33     pool_size=(2, 2),
34     strides=(2, 2)
35 ))
36
```

```
37 # Fourth convolution.
38 model.add(tf.keras.layers.Convolution2D(
39     filters=128,
40     kernel_size=3,
41     activation=tf.keras.activations.relu
42 ))
43 model.add(tf.keras.layers.MaxPooling2D(
44     pool_size=(2, 2),
45     strides=(2, 2)
46 ))
47
48 # Flatten the results to feed into dense layers.
49 model.add(tf.keras.layers.Flatten())
50 model.add(tf.keras.layers.Dropout(0.5))
51
52 # 512 neuron dense layer.
53 model.add(tf.keras.layers.Dense(
54     units=512,
55     activation=tf.keras.activations.relu
56 ))
57
58 # Output layer.
59 model.add(tf.keras.layers.Dense(
60     units=NUM_CLASSES,
61     activation=tf.keras.activations.softmax
62 ))
```

Plotting the CNN model

```
1 tf.keras.utils.plot_model(
2     model,
3     show_shapes=True,
4     show_layer_names=True,
5 )
```

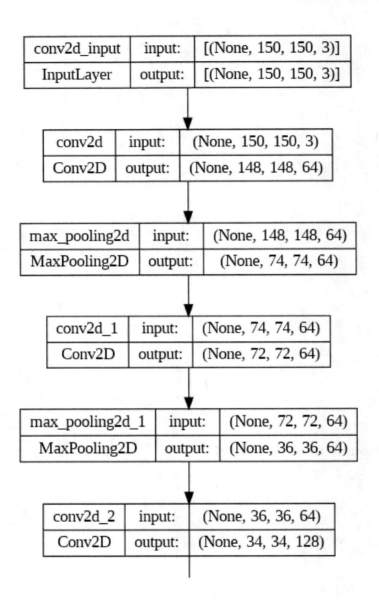

conv2d_input	input:	[(None, 150, 150, 3)]
InputLayer	output:	[(None, 150, 150, 3)]

conv2d	input:	(None, 150, 150, 3)
Conv2D	output:	(None, 148, 148, 64)

max_pooling2d	input:	(None, 148, 148, 64)
MaxPooling2D	output:	(None, 74, 74, 64)

conv2d_1	input:	(None, 74, 74, 64)
Conv2D	output:	(None, 72, 72, 64)

max_pooling2d_1	input:	(None, 72, 72, 64)
MaxPooling2D	output:	(None, 36, 36, 64)

conv2d_2	input:	(None, 36, 36, 64)
Conv2D	output:	(None, 34, 34, 128)

42

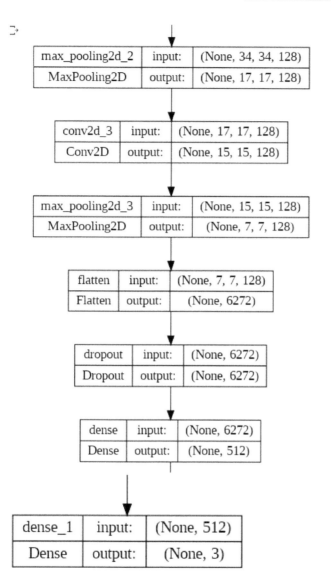

max_pooling2d_2	input:	(None, 34, 34, 128)
MaxPooling2D	output:	(None, 17, 17, 128)

conv2d_3	input:	(None, 17, 17, 128)
Conv2D	output:	(None, 15, 15, 128)

max_pooling2d_3	input:	(None, 15, 15, 128)
MaxPooling2D	output:	(None, 7, 7, 128)

flatten	input:	(None, 7, 7, 128)
Flatten	output:	(None, 6272)

dropout	input:	(None, 6272)
Dropout	output:	(None, 6272)

dense	input:	(None, 6272)
Dense	output:	(None, 512)

dense_1	input:	(None, 512)
Dense	output:	(None, 3)

COMPILING THE MODEL

The model compile () is a method in TensorFlow that prepares the model for training and evaluation by configuring it with an optimizer, loss function, and metrics. The optimizer updates the model weights during training, while the loss function measures how well the model performs during training. The metrics evaluate the performance of the model during both training and testing.

```
[37]  1 # adam_optimizer = tf.keras.optimizers.Adam(learning_rate=0.001)
      2 rmsprop_optimizer = tf.keras.optimizers.RMSprop(learning_rate=0.001)
      3
      4 model.compile(
      5     optimizer=rmsprop_optimizer,
      6     loss=tf.keras.losses.sparse_categorical_crossentropy,
      7     metrics=['accuracy']
      8 )
```

TRAINING THE MODEL

```
 1 # Preparing callbacks.
 2 os.makedirs('logs/fit', exist_ok=True)
 3 tensorboard_log_dir = 'logs/fit/' + datetime.datetime.now().strftime('%Y%m%d-%H%M%S')
 4 tensorboard_callback = tf.keras.callbacks.TensorBoard(
 5     log_dir=tensorboard_log_dir,
 6     histogram_freq=1
 7 )
 8
 9 os.makedirs('tmp/checkpoints', exist_ok=True)
10 model_checkpoint_callback = tf.keras.callbacks.ModelCheckpoint(
11     filepath='tmp/checkpoints/weights.{epoch:02d}-{val_loss:.2f}.hdf5'
12 )
13
14 early_stopping_callback = tf.keras.callbacks.EarlyStopping(
15     patience=5,
16     monitor='val_accuracy'
17     # monitor='val_loss'
18 )
```

44

We use the **model fit** () method to train our model. The x parameter identifies the input data for the training process with the dataset "train_augmented_shuffled."

The validation data parameter is the input data for the validation process; we use the "dataset_test_shuffled" dataset.

The epochs parameter indicates the number of times the model will iterate over the entire training dataset. The "steps_per_epoch" parameter specifies the number of batches of samples processed before a training epoch is complete.

The validation steps parameter shows the number of batches of samples processed before considering a validation epoch complete.

Finally, the callbacks parameter details a list of callbacks applied during training. In the code snippet, we have **"tensorboard_callback."**

```
1 training_history = model.fit(
2     x=dataset_train_augmented_shuffled.repeat(),
3     validation_data=dataset_test_shuffled.repeat(),
4     epochs=15,
5     steps_per_epoch=steps_per_epoch,
6     validation_steps=validation_steps,
7     callbacks=[
8         # model_checkpoint_callback,
9         # early_stopping_callback,
10        tensorboard_callback
11    ],
12    verbose=1
13 )
```

```
Epoch 1/15
78/78 [==============================] - 30s 223ms/step - loss: 1.1112 - accuracy: 0.3970 - val_loss: 1.0813 - val_accuracy: 0.4176
Epoch 2/15
78/78 [==============================] - 17s 214ms/step - loss: 0.7027 - accuracy: 0.7203 - val_loss: 0.6052 - val_accuracy: 0.7273
Epoch 3/15
78/78 [==============================] - 15s 200ms/step - loss: 0.4140 - accuracy: 0.8485 - val_loss: 0.5442 - val_accuracy: 0.6903
Epoch 4/15
78/78 [==============================] - 17s 219ms/step - loss: 0.2718 - accuracy: 0.9039 - val_loss: 0.8972 - val_accuracy: 0.7074
Epoch 5/15
78/78 [==============================] - 15s 197ms/step - loss: 0.1623 - accuracy: 0.9465 - val_loss: 1.4959 - val_accuracy: 0.6989
Epoch 6/15
78/78 [==============================] - 16s 208ms/step - loss: 0.1542 - accuracy: 0.9449 - val_loss: 0.7041 - val_accuracy: 0.7642
```

45

ANALYZING RESULTS

In the left graph, we analyze how the loss between the Training Set and the Test Set is smaller as we approach the end of the Epochs.

In the right graph, we analyze how the accuracy between the Training Set and the Test Set is bigger as we approach the end of the Epochs.

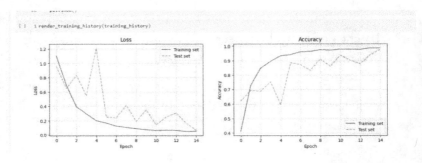

Chapter III

Principles for AI Development at Microsoft

Six principles should guide AI development:

> **Principle of Fairness.** AI systems should treat all people fairly.

> **Principle of Inclusiveness.** AI systems should empower everyone and engage people.

> **Principle of Reliability & Safety.** AI systems should perform reliably and safely.

> **Principle of Transparency.** AI systems should be understandable.

> **Principle of Privacy & Security.** AI systems should perform reliably and safely.

> **Principle of Accountability.** People should be accountable for AI systems. (**Microsoft-AI-01**)

If you plan to write Microsoft Exam AI-900, it is important to memorize these six principles and their definitions.

Case Study: Hospital Employee and Resource Optimization System (HEROS) (Microsoft-AI-02)

Microsoft posted a guide with a case study to explain how teams could use the activities to complete an Impact Assessment Template. In this assessment, you can find an AI system that optimizes healthcare resources, the allocation of hospital beds, and employee scheduling.

The AI system predicts the patient's stay in the hospital and provides bed allocation and staff scheduling. The system input includes patient medical data and staff scheduling parameters.

The data training of the AI system from a specific hospital included:

- The medical history of the patients.
- The type of surgery that patients had at the hospital.
- Hospital stays in the hospital.
- Historic employment and scheduling data.

This AI system is the "Hospital Employee and Resource Optimization System" (HEROS). This hospital system helps manage the allocation of hospital beds and the scheduling of staff shifts.

System Profile Guidance

Microsoft summarized the AI system Impact Assessment in the lines below. Every AI system Impact Assessment should have the following sections:

System description Guidance.

This section helps readers understand what exactly you are building. It explains what kind of AI capabilities the system has. Write it using simple language and be specific in describing the AI concepts.

Here are the topics you should include in this section:

- What are you building?
- What does it do?
- How does it work?

System purpose Guidance

This section helps readers to understand why you are building this system.

This statement should include the following topics:

- Who is the end user or primary customer of the system?
- How did the user complete this task today?
- What is the value that the system will provide?

System features Guidance

This section helps readers understand the capabilities of the system. Describe here the system's features and capabilities in general.

Geographic areas and languages Guidance

When planning the system, you should know the geographic areas where the AI system will or will not work. This approach helps maintain fairness by aiding the identification of the demographic groups and languages to guarantee the detection of fairness issues to mitigate them.

Deployment mode Guidance

This section helps readers to understand how the AI system implementation works for users or customers.

The solutions may include the following services:

• Online Services

- Platform Services

- Coding

- On Premises

- Container

How do you identify system uses?

Follow the following activity steps:

1) Brainstorm identifies the potential ways someone could use the system, no matter how unusual they seem.

2) Categorize the possible types of AI use:

- Intended
- Unsupported
- Misused

For each usage you listed in the brainstorm, determine the kind of use, intended, unsupported, or misuse of the system.

AI-900

Microsoft has the exam AI-900: Microsoft Azure AI Fundamentals exam. Applicants for this exam should have a solid knowledge of machine learning (ML) and artificial intelligence (AI) concepts. Coding knowledge is not necessary to pass this exam; the ML scenarios run on Azure.

AI-900 Exam

The AI-900 exam covers the following topics:

- Describe AI workloads and considerations (20-25%)

- Describe fundamental principles of machine learning on Azure (25-30%)

- Describe features of computer vision workloads on Azure (15-20%)

- Describe features of Natural Language Processing (NLP) workloads on Azure (25-30%)

Udemy AI-900 course

Udemy offers the course Learn Azure Artificial Intelligence and Machine Learning (ML) technologies" by

Scott Duffy. It is an excellent course to prepare for the AI-900 exam.

I have added a bank of questions prepared with Coop Student Musab in his Project "The AI bank to generate quizzes randomly."

QR ONE

PART II

Chapter IV

AI in Manufacturing

(Silva-Zapata, Manufacturing Workshop 2019)

The industrial revolution 1.0 started at the end of the 18th century. This revolution brought significant transformations that changed the existing economies in Europe at this stage.

The periods of the industrial revolution 1.0 to 4.0 were:

First industrial revolution: Industry 1.0

In 1784 Edmund Cartwright designed and patented the first mechanical loom that helped the industrialization of weaving for the textile industry.

Second industrial revolution: Industry 2.0

In 1870 First production and assembly lines were used in Cincinnati, Ohio, slaughterhouses for the meat industry. In 1913 these techniques inspired Henry Ford to design automobile assembly lines.

Third industrial revolution: Industry 3.0

In 1969 the First programmable logic controller (PLC), Modicon 084, helped automate processes and gather and share data.

Fourth industrial revolution: Industry 4.0

Since 2010, Industry 4.0 has been transforming how companies manufacture, improve, and supply products. Companies are integrating state-of-the-art technologies, incorporating the Internet of Things (IoT), Cloud Technology, Artificial Intelligence (AI), Machine Learning (ML), 3D Printing, Industrial Automation, and Advanced Robotics into their production facilities and throughout their operations.

A smart factory is a system that uses artificial intelligence (AI) and machine learning (ML) to examine data, drive programmed processes, and learn.

Intelligent factories have advanced devices, embedded software, and robotics that gather and evaluate data, permitting better management. Nevertheless, the system generates higher value by combining data from production and operations with operational data from Enterprise Resource Planning (ERP), supply chain, and customer service to establish unique levels. of visibility and understanding.

Smart factories provide an excellent opportunity for industries to enter the fourth industrial revolution. Examining the abundant amount of data collected from sensors in the factory permits real-time visibility of manufacturing resources. It can provide tools for implementing predictive maintenance to minimize equipment downtime.

All industrial companies can use Industry 4.0 models and technologies.

Here you have a PowerPoint slide that shows the periods of the industrial revolution 1.0 to 4.0.

The following table shows the trends of the Compound Annual Growth Rate (CAGR) of the different technologies used in Industry 4.0.

Transformational Force	Compound Annual Growth Rate (CAGR) by 2030
Internet of Things (IoT)	24.91% from 2023 to 2030 to reach $ 1,520 billion
Cloud Technology	14% from 2023 to 2030 to reach $ 1,600 billion
Artificial Intelligence (AI)	53.4% from 2023 to 2030 to reach $ 2,000 billion
3D printing technology	23.3% from 2023 to 2030 to reach $ 88.2 billion
Industrial Automation Market	23.3% from 2023 to 2030 to reach $ 399 billion
Robotic Process Automation	30.76% from 2023 to 2030 to reach $ 25.83 billion
Cyber-physical system	10.59% from 2023 to 2030 to reach $ 15.56 billion
Global Augmented reality	29.50% from 2023 to 2030 to reach $ 164.0 billion
Big data and analytics	13.2% from 2023 to 2030 to reach $ 252.4 million

Internet of Things (IoT)

IoT, known as the Internet of Things, is a network of devices, machines, buildings, motor vehicles, and other items connected to electronic sensors with software that connects them, enabling these objects to collect and exchange data.

Cloud Technology

Cloud Technology uses remote data centers, where the data is stored in servers to manage process data that the users retrieve through the Internet.

AI

AI helps power efficiencies in manufacturing by managing complex inventory, quality, suppliers, and production processes. It allows robots and personnel to collaborate to accomplish tasks and take on more repetitive tasks.

AI systems will improve processes' speed, precision, and quality control. There are two specific areas where AI will excel: forecasting and understanding anomalies or outliers.

3D Printing Technology (Britannica 2023).

"**3D printing**, in full three-dimensional printing, in manufacturing, any of several processes for fabricating three-dimensional objects by layering two-dimensional cross sections sequentially, one on top of another."

3D printing is known as additive manufacturing because it involves building objects from the bottom up.

Industrial Automation Market

Additive Manufacturing is a computer-controlled process that creates three-dimensional objects by depositing materials in layers.

Global Robotic Process Automation

In advanced robotics, robots are programmable machines that can conduct tasks autonomously.

Cyber-physical system

Cyber security defends computers, servers, mobile devices, electronic systems, networks, and data from malicious attacks.

Each IoT sensor, hub, and network has an IP address to communicate with the Manufacturing System. The network in a smart factory must be isolated and protected from external intruders with the proper protocols, routers, and software.

Global Augmented reality

Technology creates an enhanced version of the natural world, adding digital information.

Augmented reality allows users to have punctual information about the different modules in a machine. It describes what is the use or limits of each piece.

Big Data and Analytics

There is an extensive collection of structured and unstructured data in each business; for example, in the banks, all the transactions their customers make in the ATMs are enormous. In other industries like manufacturing, each process and machinery around them produces every second different raw data.

These Big data is collected, examined, and analyzed to discover trends, insights, and patterns that can help businesses make effective decisions.

Communication Protocols in IoT

In smart factories, the first communication protocols used for IoT are:

- Wi-Fi protocol is suitable in LAN networks, allowing fast data transfer.
- Bluetooth protocol is appropriate for short-range communication between devices.
- Ethernet/IP is an industrial network protocol from the standard Ethernet.
- Zigbee is a protocol for devices with low power and low band.
- MQTT (Message Queuing Telemetry Transport) is a lightweight, machine-to-machine network protocol.
- Cellular data is suitable for long-distance wireless communications.

63

Here you have additional protocols used in IoT:

- Microsoft Azure has RTOS (real-time operating system) security protocol for IoT for embedded devices to connect an application to the Cloud.
- Azure uses Azure Defender for IoT addresses, and IP/MAC address mapping to the communication between devices in the network. (Microsoft, Develop secure embedded applications with Azure RTOS 2022)
- Samsung Electronics signed in March 2023 a partnership with IBM to combine AI IBM with private 5G networks. This new system will analyze big data with 5G high-speed data transfer in the collection data center before sending it to the Cloud. (Telecom.com 2023)

IBM and Siemens have worked together on different IoT projects. Siemens' industrial IoT-as-a-service solution and Mindsphere, an IoT analytics solution from Siemens, combined with IBM's Cloud, helped deploy intelligent solutions. **(Decisions 2021)**.

IBM has the Red Hat OpenShift system, an enterprise **Kubernetes platform** that combines tested and trusted services to manage applications smoothly. Mindsphere runs in IBM Cloud to optimize applications in IoT.

Closed-Loop Manufacturing

(SIEMENS Team 2019)

When I attended UNI University in Peru, I took Control I and Control II courses, where we learned the Laplace formulas, Nyquist Locus, and closed loops with feedback.

I first applied this theory at OSELK, repairing Temperature and Speed controllers and adjusting the gain potentiometers to set the temperature or speed stability.

When we designed an AVR (Automatic Voltage Regulator) to control the voltage generated by the Alternators from Diesel groups, that test was a different challenge where the alternator power could reach four hundred Kilowatts in the system.

In Python Robotics, I simulated real robots with closed-loop feedback.

When I learned about the Digital twins, I understood the principle that Siemens, Microsoft, Google, and IBM have created.

First, we will start learning what a Digital Twin is and what pieces form the closed loop in the systems.

Digital Twins

It is a digital model of a physical product, system, or process (known as the physical system) that operates as the digital counterpart for synchronization, updating and verifying data, and improving performance to optimize the processes. It is a virtual model of physical systems.

A digital twin works in real-time and synchronizes with the corresponding physical system.

Closed-Loop

Enterprise resource planning (ERP) systems by 1990 used this platform to manage and integrate sales, accounting, engineering, and HR (Human resources) in different businesses.

Integrating these ERP systems into operations and production in manufacturing has been a big challenge. The massive amount of data obtained from these areas connects instant data to the ERP platform to improve processes, production, and revenues. The feedback of this data to the platform is known as closed loop.

In manufacturing, there are now known Manufacturing ERP platforms:

- Microsoft Dynamics 365 Business Central: It connects sales, finance, service, and operations to optimize supply change management.

- Oracle NetSuite: is a cloud-based ERP solution that helps manufacturers control, coordinate, and manage every aspect of their operations in one place.

  - SAP (Systems, Applications, and Products). It now has SAP MII (Manufacturing Integration and Intelligence) solution. It connects the supply chain to manufacturing operations, production, processes, equipment, and people.

  - Siemens Manufacturing Execution System (MES). It works with the different modules MOM (Manufacturing Operations Management), ERP, and PLM (Product Lifecycle Management)

Here is information about Digital Twins at Google, Microsoft, and Siemens.

Digital Twins at Google

Google Cloud launched in September 2021 a new digital twin service for supply chain systems.

Google uses BigQuery in a supply chain model; it uses BigQuery to analyze data from various sources such as enterprise business systems (ERP), IoT devices, and other data sources. You can then use the insights gained from this analysis to optimize your supply chain operations.

For example, you can use BigQuery to analyze data from your ERP system to identify product demand trends. You can then use this information to optimize your inventory levels and ensure you have enough stock to meet customer demand.

Google Cloud also has its own Supply Chain Twin solution that allows them to build a digital representation of their existent supply chain and provides end-to-end visibility across the supply chain.

It uses its Pulse module to analyze data and display detailed real-time information.

There is an excellent explanation about this topic in the link **(Google 2022)**. The image below is a screenshot of this video.

Supply Chain Twin: A digital representation of your end-to-end supply chain

Digital Twins at Microsoft

Microsoft has developed its platform as a service (Paas) for the Digital Twins in Azure Digital Twins.

Azure Digital Twins uses a new modeling language to create the models of business processes called DTDL (Digital Twins Definition Language). Another tool is **3D Scenes Studio** which helps build the twin models graphically.

It is vital to maintain the security of the transmitted data and the protocols used.

Azure IoT (Internet of Things) Hub connects the input from business and IoT devices connected in the different machines of the manufacturing process.

The insights that Azure Digital Twins extract from the data help to get better products and optimize operations and costs.

Microsoft partners in manufacturing have applied Digital Twin technology to optimize their processes.

There is more information on Digital Twins at **(Microsoft, Microsoft-Azure Digital Twins 2021)**

In the next pictures there are two different projects in 3D Scenes Studio, International Space Station, and Robotic Arms in a Factory.

INTERNATIONAL SPACE STATION (3D Scenes Studio)

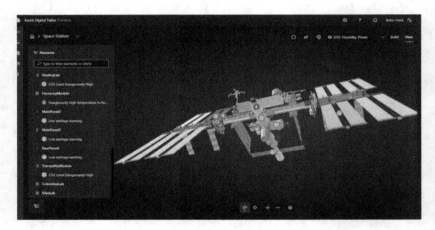

INTERNATIONAL SPACE STATION

(IoT 2022)

There is an interview with Oliver Bloch to Alex Hayward at Microsoft Learn IoT. Alex tells how he built the International Space Station (ISS) twin.

It is incredible how Alex collected IIS live telemetry information to build the IoT model.

Alex and his team implemented this Digital Twin in 3d Scenes Studio.

Here ais a picture of the International Space Station:
NASA International Space Station (NASA 2023)

"This view of the International Space Station was taken by NASA astronaut Stephen Hoburg as he worked on the Starboard-6 truss structure during a spacewalk.**"**

ROBOTIC ARMS IN A FACTORY

This project in 3D Scenes Studio has a factory section with six robotic arms. Each robotic arm has an associated Digital Twin in Azure Digital Twins that monitors the efficiency of each robotic arm; they pick up boxes and move them to other places. If the robots miss a container, the system will register the box serial number and the time of occurrence.

ROBOTIC ARMS IN A FACTORY (3D Scenes Studio)

Digital Twins at Siemens. *(SIEMENS Team 2019)*

Here you have definitions of key words in the following lines of the SIEMENS article of the above reference. The two pictures below are snapshots of the same Siemens Team 2019 article.

DEFINITIONS:

BOM: Bill of Materials

BOP: Bill of Process

CLM: **Closed-loop Manufacturing** enables firms to synchronize and optimize production across product design, production planning, manufacturing execution, automation, and intelligence from consumer use. CLM focuses on synchronizing highly efficient production of the current product.

CLQ: Closed loop Quality is a continuous process of plan-do-check-act, evaluating the quality of the product at each stage of the product's ideation. CLQ focuses on improving the quality of the product across the entire product lifecycle.

CPM: Common Plant Model

ERP: Enterprise Resource Planning

LA: Lifecycle Analytics aggregates intelligence across the entire product lifecycle, serving it in contextually relevant functions to improve quality and performance.

MDM: Master Data Model

MES: Manufacturing Execution Systems

MOM: Manufacturing Operations Management is the real-time software layer that links PLM to automation, synchronizing the virtual world of product development with the real world of production.

PLM: Product Lifecycle Management is the key to converting new ideas to marketable products faster. PLM solutions weave the necessary digital thread along all development and manufacturing phases.

TIA: Totally Integrated Automation enables seamless horizontal interoperability between automation technologies and vertical data integration from the field to the enterprise level.

DIGITAL TWINS: (SIEMENS Team 2019)

Data must be always identified and translated from one domain to the other for the digital twins to understand the information transmitted via the digital thread. The manufacturing master data model (MDM) and the common plant model (CPM) automatically link the virtual and real worlds.

(SIEMENS Team 2019) Digital Twins

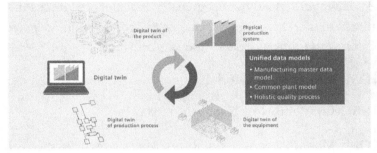

Finally, we look at the heart of closed-loop manufacturing. The MOM portfolio is used to orchestrate all the other pieces of the technology infrastructure to create the intended product for the user. MES orchestrates and controls all parts of the production process. It also ties to all the other parts of the value chain and the innovation chain. Quality is a big part of MOM and ensures the product's quality. It also ties into the larger cross lifecycle quality process of CLQ. Advanced planning and scheduling (APS) translate demand into production planning. Electronic manufacturing intelligence (EMI) is the source of the as-built data for the larger performance and quality management. TIA is the interface to smart machines. These functions need to operate in concert for digital transformation to occur.

74

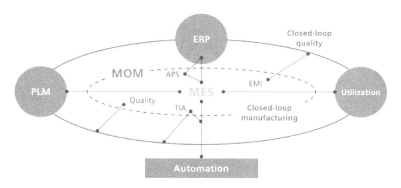

(SIEMENS Team 2019) Block Diagram of MES (Manufacturing Execution Systems)

MANUFACTURING AT IBM

IBM has been working on IoT and blockchain for the last eight years. IBM Blockchain enables business partners to share and access IoT data with maximum security. IBM Watson IoT Platform provides a fully managed, cloud-hosted service that supports IoT devices.

"IBM has been involved with Digital Twins since the Apollo space program. IBM's Real-Time Computer Complex (RTCC) was an IBM computing and data processing system at NASA's Manned Spacecraft Center in Houston. It collected, processed, and sent to Mission Control information that directed every phase of an Apollo mission." **(IBM 2019)**

QR II

PART III

Omar Silva-Fulchi   AI   <u>info@robo-geek.ca</u>

Chapter V

Machine Learning (ML)

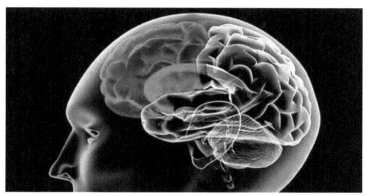

(Silva-Zapata, STEM Neural Networks 2016)

The Brain

The number of neurons in the brain is around one hundred billion, about twelve times the world population. Your brain uses all these neurons to process your Tots (thoughts).

You have over 100,000 miles of axons in your brain; daily, you have more than 70,000 Tots. That is the reason it is exceedingly difficult to focus.

The speed of nerve impulses varies enormously in diverse types of neurons. The fastest travels at about 400 Kmph.

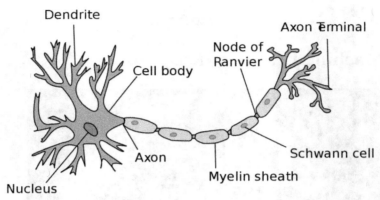

Dendrite

Axon Terminal

Node of Ranvier

Cell body

Axon

Schwann cell

Myelin sheath

Nucleus

NEURONS

Neurons transmit messages to each other with a type of electrical signal. Sensors bring information to the brain from your neurons when you see, smell, and hear. Other electrical signals come from your organs, muscles, and glands.

Neurons receive messages through their dendrites to the soma. Next, the signal leaves the soma and travels down the axon to another neuron.

The brain consists of many neurons, which are connected and communicate between them. If you think about the structure of a biological neural network, scientists observed a couple of essential properties. One was that these neurons are connected and receive electrical signals, so one neuron can propagate electrical signals to another.

Neurons process those input signals and then can activate new neurons. At one point, they can propagate further signals onto neurons.

Now we could take this biological idea of how humans learn-- with brains and neurons-- and apply that to a machine, designing an artificial neural network, which will be a mathematical model for learning.

Artificial neural networks will allow us to model mathematical functions. Every time you look at a neural network, each one is just a mathematical function that maps specific inputs to respective outputs based on the network's structure, depending on where we place the units inside this neural network. That establishes how the network is going to function.

Artificial neural networks will contribute to learning the network's parameters. We want to model such that it is easy to write code allowing the network to figure out how to model the correct mathematical function given a particular input data set.

.

Neuron Model

In the Neuron Model below, the artificial neuron multiplies the inputs with the corresponding weights, then summarizes the products and compares the sum with the threshold. The most used equation for this case is the sigmoid function. To obtain the y output, apply the x value to the threshold function.

Neural Network Types

We will learn about the following type of neural networks:

- Feed-forward neural networks,
- Convolutional neural networks, and
- Recurrent neural networks.

Let us imagine we provide an image as input into our neural network, and the neural network will generate an output describing the image.

This problem would pose a challenge for traditional feed-forward neural networks because we have a fixed-size input and a fixed-size output in these neural networks.

The size of the inputs, the number of values in the input, and the number of values in the output will constantly be constant based on the neural network's structure.

It is challenging for a neural network to take an image and describe the scene in text because the output is a sequence of words. Depending on the image, the output can have different numbers of words. However, certain types of neural networks can manage variable-sized datasets, such as Recurrent Neural Networks (RNNs) and their variant, Long Short-Term Memory (LSTM) networks.

We could have sequences of different lengths and still want to generate the appropriate output. The strategy here is to use a recurrent neural network, which can feed its output back into itself as input for the next time.

There is a one-to-many relationship between inputs to outputs. These are what we consider to be one-to-one neural networks-- you pass in one set of values as input, and you get one vector of values as the output-- but in this case, we want to pass in one value as input-- the image–, and we want to get a sequence-- many values-- as output, where each value is like one of these words that get produced by this algorithm.

We are going to train the network to output what the first word of the caption should be. However, the result will only be part of the sequence of words because we can only represent part of the sequence of words. Instead, the output is just going to be the first word. We are using just a fixed set of neurons.

Right now, because the network generates output that can be fed back into itself, you can imagine the output of the network being delivered back into the same network-- this here looks like a separate network, but it is the same network that is just getting different input-- that this network's output gets fed back into itself.

Even now, it is going to generate another output, and that output is going to be like the second word in the caption. This recurrent neural network will generate other output that enters itself to create another word.

Recurrent neural networks allow us to represent this sort of one-to-many structure. We provide one image as input, and the neural network can pass data into the next run of the network, and then again and again, such that you could run the network multiple times, each time generating a different output, still based on that original input.

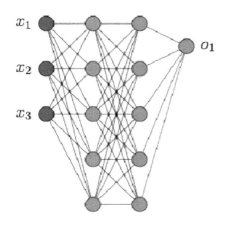

RECURRENT NEURAL NETWORK (RNN)

Recurrent neural networks become particularly useful when dealing with sequences of inputs or outputs. Our output is a sequence of words, and since we can't very quickly represent outputting an entire line of words.

We will instead output that sequence one word at a time by allowing our network to pass information about what still needs to be explained about the photo into the next stage of running the networks.

We could run the network multiple times-- the same network with the same weights-- just getting different inputs each time, first getting information from the image and then from the neural network.

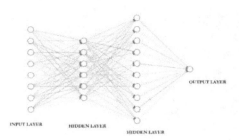

CONVOLUTIONAL NEURAL NETWORK

We could use neural networks to analyze images in the context of convolutional neural networks that take a photo, figure out different properties of the image, and can draw conclusions based on that. This process is many one-to-many relationships inside of a recurrent neural network.

YouTube needs to be able to learn a lot based on a video; they need to look through videos to detect copyright violations or identify what items are inside the video. Video data is more challenging to put as input to a neural network because, whereas in an image, we can treat each pixel as a different value, videos are sequences.

They are sequences of images, and each series might be an extra length, so it might be challenging to represent that entire video as a single vector of values that you could pass into a neural network.

Recurrent neural networks can be a valuable solution for trying to solve this type of problem. Then instead of just passing in a single input into our neural network, we could pass in the input one frame at a time, taking the first frame of the video and passing it into the network.

Let us take in another input and, this time, pass it into the network, but the network gets information from the last time we provided input into the network. Then we pass in a third and a fourth input, where each time the network gets the most recent intake, like each video frame, it also receives the information the network processed from all previous iterations.

Therefore, on frame number four, we get the input for frame number four plus the network's data calculated from the first three frames. This recurrent neural network can also learn to extract patterns from a data sequence using all the data frames.

If we want to categorize a video into different categories, such as educational videos, music videos, or other types of videos, you can use a classification task where you take input from each video frame and output something like what it is and what category it belongs to.

If we have a sequence as input, you can use many-to-one learning to categorize it. For example, if you have a movie review and want to classify it as positive or negative, you can use the words in the review as input, and the output would be the classification.

A recurrent neural network can help analyze sequences of words, which is useful when dealing with language. For example, if you have a series of words as input and want to classify it as positive or negative, the output would be the classification.

We can also use this approach for spoken language. Spoken language is an audio waveform segmented into distinct chunks, and each of those chunks passes as input into a recurrent neural network to classify someone's voice. For example, we can use this method if we want to do voice recognition to identify one person or another.

We can use many types of neural networks for different computations. The long short-term memory neural network (LSTM) is one of the most popular types of recurrent neural networks and can be powerful when dealing with sequences, especially sequences of words when dealing with natural language.

Adversarial networks are another type of neural network where networks compete to try and generate new kinds of data, and other networks can solve other tasks based on what they happen to be structured and adapted for.

Machine learning tools are practical for learning rapidly based on input data to figure out how to calculate the functions, from inputs to outputs. These tools have many applications for machine learning, whether it is input to some classification like analyzing an image and getting a digit or machine translation where the information is in one language and the output is in another.

Machine Learning (ML)

(Silva-Zapata, RG-680 - ML 2018)

The **Machine Learning (ML)** algorithm is a program. It includes instructions for pattern discovery within the provided data set.

There are three ML groups:

The **Supervised group** makes predictions based on the information from the prior results (labeled data).

The Supervised model types depend on structured data, where the input columns or fields are the features, and the output is the label or labels.

There are two Supervised model types:

The **Regression model** produces a numeric value prediction for the label, the higher the score, the better the model.

Regression

Every time we predict values in Supervised learning, we utilize Regressions.

For example, predicting house market values or students' marks.

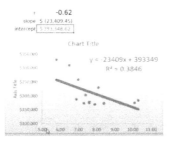

The **Classification model** predicts a class (car or truck) or multi-class (car, truck, or van) of the label based on incoming data (features).

For example, predicting if an image contains a car or a truck.

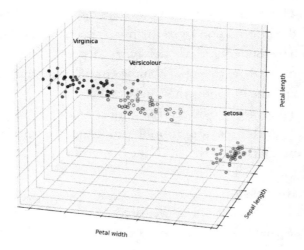

An **Unsupervised group** makes predictions without prior knowledge of the possible outcomes.

- The Clustering model belongs to the Unsupervised model type. This model predicts which data points belong to the cluster or group.
- The Clustering algorithm learns from the data the common cluster properties. Then computes the cluster membership and probability for each data point.

The **Reinforced group** learns from the result and chooses the next move based on this knowledge.

90

Azure ML Metrics

Azure ML uses model evaluation for the measurement of the trained model accuracy.

Azure ML uses these metrics:

- MAE (Mean absolute error) measures the errors between predicted and observed values. The lower the score, the better the model performance.
- MSE (Mean Squared Error)
- The MSE measures the square error between the predicted and the true target values.
- The mean squared error (MSE) determines the distance between the set of points and the regression line by taking the distances from the collection of points to the regression line and then swapping them. Distances are nothing but errors.

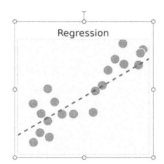

$$MSE = \frac{1}{n} \sum_{i=1}^{n} (y_i - \tilde{y}_i)^2$$

RMSE (Root Mean Squared Error) represents the square root from the squared mean of the errors between predicted and actual values.

RSE (Relative squared error) measures the square of the differences between predicted and actual values. The value is between 0 and 1. The closer this value is to 0, the better is model performance.

RAE (Relative absolute error) measures differences between predicted and actual values. The value is between 0 and 1. The closer this value is to 0, the better is model performance.

R (R CORRELATION FACTOR)

One of the most used formulas is Pearson's correlation coefficient formula. This is the formula used to get the r collection factor:

$$r = \frac{n(\Sigma xy) - (\Sigma x)(\Sigma y)}{\sqrt{[\,n\Sigma x^2 - (\Sigma x)^2\,]\,[\,n\Sigma y^2 - (\Sigma y)^2\,]}}$$

The **R-squared model** describes how well the combination of the independent variables as a single unit explains the target variable. The R-squared value ranges between 1 and 0. Its represented by the below formula:

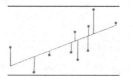

$$R^2 = 1 - \frac{SS_{RES}}{SS_{TOT}} = 1 - \frac{\sum_i (y_i - \hat{y}_i)}{\sum_i (y_i - \overline{y})}$$

Building the Model in ML

There are four steps to building a model in ML:

- Select and prepare a training data set necessary to solve the problem. There are two types of data labeled or unlabeled.
- Choose an algorithm to run on the training data.
- If the data type is labeled, the algorithm could be regression, decision trees, or instance based.
- If the data type is unlabeled, the algorithm could be a clustering algorithm, an association algorithm, or a neural network.
- Train the algorithm to create the model.
- Use and improve the model.

Building Machine Learning solutions with Azure

Here you have the tasks for building Machine Learning solutions with Azure:

1. **Data ingestion.**

Data ingestion brings data from different sources into a shared repository or storage. After ingestion, data is accessible for various services.

There are three general ways to get the data:

- Upload a dataset,
- manual input,
- And import data.

Azure ML Studio has four options for importing data:

- From local files,
- From datastore,
- From web files,

- and From Open Datasets.

2. **Data preparation and data transformation**.

Before using the data for Machine Learning modeling, we must prepare or pre-process data:

Find and correct data errors,

Remove outliers. A piece of data that is very different from all the others in a set.

Assign missing data with appropriate data values.

It is essential to have clean data before we build our ML models.

Azure Auto ML executes data preparation during the run.

Azure ML Designer provides different modules for correcting the data:

- Clip Values (for outliers),
- Clean Missing Data (for missing data),
- Remove Duplicate Rows,
- Apply SQL Transformation to the data, Python, and R scripts.

3. **Feature selection and engineering.**

Before model training, we must review the data, select features that influence the prediction (label), and discard other elements from the final dataset.

If the dataset has numeric fields on different scales, one column has all values from 0 to 10 and another from 1000 to 4000. We must bring them to a standard scale.

This process is known as data normalization.

This operation is known as feature engineering if the ML solution generates a new feature based on the current elements for better model performance.

Users can script these operations using SQL Transformation, Python, and R modules.

In Azure ML, featurization is the name for the generic application of all data-preprocessing techniques, like scaling, normalization, or feature engineering.

4. Model training.

After data preprocessing, data is practically ready for model training. We need to have two sets of data: one for training and one for test or validation.

Auto ML splits the original dataset into training and validation sets automatically. However, users have the option to upload a validation set.

Azure ML Designer provides a Split Data module for
creating training and test datasets.

Before the training, we need to connect the left output of a Split Data module to a Training module's correct input.

We must also connect the selected solution ML Algorithm module to the Training module's left input. For Regression and Classification models, we need to mark a label column in the Training module. And we can run the training.

95

5. Evaluation.

Auto ML uses a validation dataset for model validation and cross-validation of the child processes. After you finish the training, we need to score (test) a model with the test dataset.

Azure ML Designer utilizes the Score Model module to achieve the model predictions using the test dataset. The score results from passes to the Evaluate Model module.

The module evaluates the score results and produces the standard model performance metrics.

6. Model deployment.

We can deploy the model to a production environment if the model performance is satisfactory. For model deployment, do we need to create the production version of the training Pipeline?

Inference pipeline. Azure ML Designer provides an option to create a real-time inference pipeline. After we complete the inference
pipeline, we need to do the test run. But before that, we want to be sure that our input field selection doesn't include a labeled field.

We are ready to deploy our solution if the inference pipeline test run is successful. For the next step, we must have Inference Clusters provisioned. We can only push the Deploy button in the Azure ML Designer's top right to deploy the solution.

After deployment, we can see the solution's status on the Assets section's Azure ML Studio Endpoints blade.

7. Model management.

Azure ML implements principles from DevOps for model maintenance. This approach is Machine Learning Operations.

It includes reproducible environments, code management, package deployment, monitoring, alerts, notification, and end-to-end automation.

Chapter VI

Computer Vision (CV)

Azure's Computer Vision service gives you access to algorithms used to process images; the system returns data based on the visual features you want. Computer Vision is one of the critical elements of Artificial Intelligence.

It includes the following services:

- Computer vision analyzes images and video, detects objects and text, extracts descriptions, and creates tags.
- Custom vision trains custom models for image classification and custom object detection.
- Face detects, analyzes, and recognizes faces.
- Form Recognizer extracts information from scanned forms and invoices.
- Video Indexer analyzes and indexes video and audio content.

Computer vision service works with images. This service brings sense to the image pixels by using them as features for ML models. These predefined models help categorize and classify images, detect, and recognize objects, and tag, and identify them.

Computer vision can "read" a text in images in 25 languages and recognize landmarks.

Azure Cognitive Face service currently includes the following functionality:

- Face detection,
- Face verification,
- Find similar faces,
- The group faces similarities,
- and Person identification.

Face API service calls return Face Attributes. Face Attributes include:

- Age,
- Gender,
- Smile,
- Glasses (Reading glasses),
- Emotions (anger, contempt, disgust, fear, happiness, neutral, sadness, surprise),
- Makeup (eye makeup, lip makeup),
- Facial Hair (Moustache, beard, sideburns)

The Form Recognizer service in Azure uses pre-build receipt models to obtain information from receipts:

- date of transaction,
- time of the transaction,
- merchant information,
- taxes paid,
- receipt total.

The service also recognizes all text on the receipt and returns it.

Custom Vision service helps create your computer vision model. These models use image classifications. As for any classification model, it should be a set of images for each known class or category.

Custom Vision service **relies on deep learning techniques**. These techniques use convolutional neural networks (CNN). CNN links pixels to the classes or categories.

Users can create the Custom Vision solution using an available Azure Cognitive Service resource. It includes both resources for training and prediction. Or they can create separate Custom Vision resources only for training or prediction.

Such separation is valid only for resource-tracking purposes. After provisioning the resources, users train the model at the Custom Vision portal: **https://www.customvision.ai**.

Here they can create applications and submit images. It should be enough images with object classes from various angles.

101

When you create a model, the service assesses its performance based on the following metrics:

- -Precision defines the percentage of the correct class predictions the model makes. For example, if the model predicts ten images are cars, and there are only seven cars, the model precision is 70% (7/10) x 100).
- Recall defines the percentage of the correct class identification the model makes. For example, if there are ten robot images, and the model identifies only eight, the model recall is 80% (8/10) x 100).
- The Average Precision (AP) calculates its metrics with the precision and the Recall values.

For automated document processing, Form Recognizer uses two models:

- Custom Model and
- A pre-built receipt model.

With the Custom model approach, you train the Form Recognizer model based on your form and data. You need only five samples of your document to start.

A pre-build receipt model is a Form Recognizer default model trained to work with receipts. It helps recognize receipts and extract data from them.

Chapter VII

Natural Language Processing (NLP)

Natural Language Processing (NLP) is one important element of Artificial Intelligence.

Microsoft Azure Cognitive Services includes four services:

Text Analytics can help you analyze text documents by detecting the language, extracting key phrases, and determining entities. It can also provide sentiment analysis.

Translator Text can translate texts in real-time between 70+ languages.

Speech Recognition can help you recognize and synthesize speech, identify speakers, and translate live or recorded speech.

Language Understanding Intelligent Service (LUIS), which can help you understand voice or text commands.

Azure Cognitive services provide two types of Translation:

Text and Speech. Azure Translator service supports multi-language near real-time text translations between 70 languages.

The service uses neural network technologies.

Custom Translator extends Translator with custom-specific language domains.

Custom extended models can benefit both Translator and Speech services for their translations. Users can easily integrate Translator and Custom Translator with their applications.

It is important to know that the Translator doesn't store any user's data.

If we need to translate the same text into other languages simultaneously, we can do it in one request to API.

We submit a text for Translation in the API call body and a sequence of the language codes for Translation as parameters.

Azure Translator service supports multi-language translations between **70 languages**.

It uses **Neural Machine Translation** (NMT) technology as a service backbone. The significant benefit of NMT is that it assesses the entire sentence before translating the words.

Custom Translator customizes NMT systems for Translation of the specific domain terminology.

The translator Text API service has two options for fine-tuning the results: -

Profanity filtering controls a translation of profanity words by marking them as profanity or omitting them. —

Selective Translation allows users to tag a word or phrase we don't need to translate, like a brand name.

The biggest language processing challenge is understanding the meaning of the text or speech. The language understanding models resolve this issue.

Azure Language Understanding service, or LUIS, helps users to work with language models.

The primary goal of LUIS-based applications is to understand the **user's intention**.

LUIS examines the user's input or utterance and extracts the keywords or entities. It then uses a compiled list of entities linked to intent and outputs the probable action or tasks the user wants to execute.

The LUIS portal (https://www.luis.ai) provided by Azure can help you create solutions based on language models.

105

There are two stages in this process: authoring and prediction. Authoring is the process of creating and training a language understanding model. To train these models, we need to supply the following key elements:

An **entity** is a word or phrase that is the focus of the utterance, as the word "flight" in the utterance "Book a flight."

Intent is the action or task that the user wants to execute. It reflects in utterance as a goal or purpose. In natural language processing, we can define intent as "Book a flight" in the utterance "Book a flight to Lima."

An **utterance** is the user's input that your model needs to interpret, such as "Book a flight to Lima" or "Book a flight."

There are four types of entities that we can create:

Machine-Learned,

List,

RegEx and

Pattern Any.

We can use pre-built LUIS collections of intents and entities for common domains such as schedules, locations, and Services for our model.

After defining the intents and entities, we can iteratively train our model using sample utterances. Once satisfied with the model performance, we can publish the LUIS application.

Every LUIS model has the default: None intent.

It is empty by default, and we can't delete it. These intent matches utterances outside of the application domain.

Prediction is the process of publishing and using the model.

Clients can connect to the predicted resource's endpoint by providing an authentication key. Before creating a LUIS application, users must choose what type of Azure resources they want to provide for their solution.

There are two types of resources:

The dedicated LUIS resources (authoring or prediction or both)

The General Azure Cognitive services resources are used only for predicting phrases. This flexibility helps the user manage resources and access different Cognitive services. But it adds overhead for the developers.

Azure Speech includes the following services: -

Speech-to-Text transcribes audio data into text —

Text-to-Speech synthesizes human-like voice audio data from the input text.

Speech Translation provides a real-time multi-language translation of the spoken language audio data into speech or text —

Voice Recognition recognizes and authenticates a speaker by the specific voice characteristics.

Speech recognition and Speech synthesis are parts of Azure Speech Services. These services help determine the spoken language content and generate the audio content by the synthetic voice.

Speech Recognition uses different models, but two are essential:

The Acoustic and The Language. The Acoustic model converts audio into phonemes.

The Language model matches phonemes with words.

Examples of Speech recognition applications are:

closed captions, phone calls or meetings transcripts, or text dictation.

Speech Synthesis is the opposite Service to Speech Recognition. It requires text content and the voice to vocalize the content.

It is working in reverse to the recognition.

First, **Speech Synthesis** tokenizes the text into individual words and matches them with phonetic sounds. Then it puts together the sounds into prosodic units, like phrases or sentences, and creates phonemes from them. After that, the service **converts phonemes into an audio sequence**.

Voice synthesizer outputs audio sequence. We can control voice output options using **Speech Synthesis Markup Language (SSML)**.

SSML, an XML-based language, can change the voice speed and pitch or how the service reads or the parts of the text.

We use Speech Synthesis services in areas like personal voice assistants, phone voice menus, or public announcements in airports and train stations.

Azure Voice Recognition service helps identify and verify the speakers by unique voice characteristics. Speakers train the service by using their voices, and the service creates an enrollment profile.

Based on this profile system can identify the speaker or user by their voice.

The Speaker Recognition APIs can identify speakers in voice recordings, real-time chats, and video streams.

Chapter VIII

Conversational AI

AI supports agents, or bots, that can keep a conversation in turns with the users.

Examples of such systems are Web chat AI agents, or bots, and Smart home devices that can answer your questions and act on your commands. Every organization is trying to keep its costs low. Usually, customer service is one of their expensive operations. So, the challenge is how to lower customer support costs without lowering service quality.

Microsoft Bot Framework is an open-source SDK for building chatbots and conversational applications. The framework includes tools and services that make creating intelligent bots that can understand natural language and respond to user requests easy. The Bot Framework also includes connectors that allow developers to connect their bots to various channels and services.

A bot is a software application written to perform specific tasks. They are automated and run according to their instructions without requiring human intervention.

Microsoft Bot Framework supports two models of bot integration with the Agent Engagement Platform:

Bot as an Agent

Bot as agent model incorporates the Bot on the same

level as live agents: the Bot is engaged in communications the same way as Customer support personnel. Transference protocol regulates the Bot's disengagement and transfer of the user's communication to a live person. The Bot as agent is the most straightforward model to implement.

BOT AS AN AGENT

Bot as a Proxy

The Bot as a Proxy model includes the Bot as the primary filter before the user interacts with a live agent. The Bot's logic determines when to transfer a conversation and where to route it. This model is more challenging to implement.

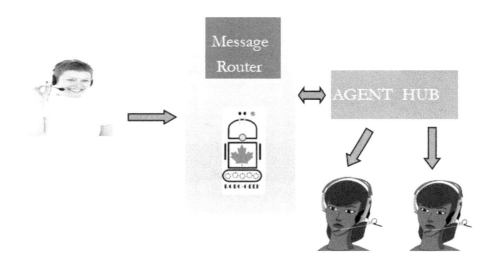

BOT AS A PROXY

A Personal Digital Assistant is a type of Bot Framework solution. A Microsoft Personal Digital Assistant is software that recognizes a user's voice and uses artificial intelligence to respond to queries.

Examples of personal digital assistants include Apple's Siri and Amazon's Alexa.

Conversational AI employs ML and NLP to collect and analyze expressions, understand them, and then make persons' responses.

> **QnA Maker**: This service helps to create a knowledge base, a foundation for a conversation between humans and AI agents.

> **Azure Bot Service**: This service helps to create, publish, and manage Conversational AI agents or bots.

Azure QnA Maker service changes semi-structured text information into structured question-and-answers pairs.

When a customer asks a question, Azure matches it with answers from the Knowledge base (KB) and outputs the most appropriate solution with a confidence score. These pairs are stored as KB. Before creating a new Knowledge base, users must provide the QnA Maker resource in their Azure subscription.

Unlike other Cognitive Services, QnA Maker relies on three Azure services.

The QnA Maker Management service is responsible for model training and publishing.

Azure Search stores data that is submitted to QnA Maker.

Azure App Service hosts QnA Maker's endpoint.

All these services are created when a QnA Maker instance is created. After resource deployment, users can create and connect a knowledge base to the model using the Azure QnA portal (https://www.qnamaker.ai/).

The portal helps populate the Knowledge base with information that comes from:

online FAQs,

product manuals,

and file documents.

Users can add **Chit-chat lists of small talk pairs** if they want to attach a personality to the conversations.

After creating a Knowledge base, users need to train and evaluate their models. Then distributed to the clients using the REST API.

Applications accessing published Knowledge base must provide the following parameters:

The KB id,

KB endpoint address,

and KB authorization key.

Users can deliver KB by creating a Bot. They also can use the QnA Maker functionality of Bot generation for their knowledge base.

Microsoft Power Virtual Agents

Power Virtual Agents is implemented as SaaS; it enables you to create chatbots with a guided, no-code graphical interface. You don't need data experts or programmers to develop your bot. It's easy to sign up and embed your bot into your website without difficulty.

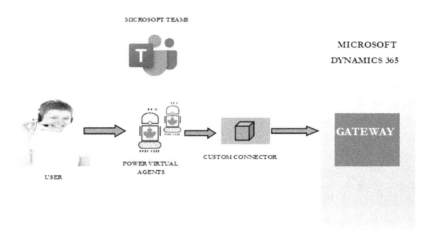

"Virtual Power Agents can be integrated with Microsoft Teams to build conversational interfaces within Teams. Users can easily and quickly build bots using a guided, no-code graphical interface. The chatbots can use the supplied standard connectors to store data stored in Microsoft Dataverse for Teams or other sources.

117

Users can add Power Virtual Agents as a discrete app from the Microsoft Teams store." **(Agent 2023)**

"Power Virtual Agents is a no-code, guided graphical interface solution that empowers every member of your team to create rich, conversational chatbots that easily integrate with the Teams platform. All content authored in Power Virtual Agents renders naturally in Teams. Power Virtual Agents bots engage with users in the Teams native chat canvas. Other chatbot creation tools include AWS Chatbot which can be primarily classified as "Chatbot Platforms &" tools" **(P. Microsoft 2020)**

To learn more about the latest news in in Power Virtual Agents, visit this Microsoft link **(P. V. Microsoft 2022)**

Watch this excellent video how to configure with Power Virtual Agent your App. **(C. i. Microsoft 2021)**

What is a REST API?

"An API, or application programming interface, is a set of rules that define how applications or devices can connect to and communicate with each other. A REST API is an API that conforms to the design principles of the REST, or representational state transfer architectural style. For this reason, REST APIs are sometimes referred to RESTful APIs". **(R. A. IBM 2020)**

HTTP REST API protocol comprises two parts:

Request and response.

A user requests an AI endpoint to process the input data. After the ML service processes the request, it responds with the results.

The request includes four key parts:

service endpoint URL,

a method,

header and a body.

Every endpoint has a service root URL, service path, and query parameters (optional).

The HTTP protocol defines the five main action methods for the service: GET, POST, PUT, PATCH, and DELETE.

The header contains the authentication key for the service and the body includes data that the user wants to process by the AI service, like the text to analyze.

We can send the request using Postman or CURL command.

The response contains the service output in JSON format.

You can get more information about REST API at **(R. A. Microsoft 2023)**

119

Chapter IX

Anomaly Detection

While working at SIMAC (Industrial Service for the Peruvian Navy), I worked on a project of vibrations measurements with my friend Victor Freundt. The Electronics lab there had state-of-the-art Brüel & Kjær equipment.

Every ship in the Navy had multiple motors, diesel engines, drive motors, propellers, auxiliary machinery, bearings, and gears onboard.

Auxiliary machinery in ships includes generators, pumps, compressors, and refrigeration systems. These systems power the ship's systems and equipment, pump water and fuel, compress air, and refrigerate food and other perishable items.

These parts in a ship generate vibrations: the engine, propeller, and shafting. Other sources of vibration include the hull and the machinery.

To measure vibrations and detect ship anomalies; SIMAC Team used B&K tools. These tools include accelerometers, amplifiers, filters used to measure the acceleration of the ship's systems and vibration meters; all this data gave the vibration levels of the ship's systems.

At the same time, we used other B&K tools to measure vibrations in the ships, like level recorders, and vibration analyzers, to analyze the vibration data collected by the accelerometers and vibration meters.

Vibration analysis examines the vibration amplitude, frequency, and phase emitted by a piece of machinery to determine the machine's functional condition.

In May, Microsoft modified the AI-900 Exam by upgrading.

its material, adding more topics in this area.

Microsoft uses Jupiter notebooks that are like the Google Colab Notebooks. It uses Python with Azure Cognitive Services for AI Anomaly Detection.

These Python notebooks show you how to use the Anomaly Detector API to detect anomalies in the data and how to visualize its returned information.

You can get information and videos about Anomaly Detection in Microsoft Learning Section at the link (Anomaly-Detection 2022).

Anomaly detection is the process of identifying unique data points or patterns that differ from the normal behavior of a data set.

We can detect anomalies in one variable with Univariate Anomaly Anomalies detection in multiple variables with Multivariate Anomaly Detection.

"When we use the API to detect anomalies, we send these three parameters:

- The API **endpoint** you named previously in Azure.

- **subscription_key** you got earlier in Azure.

- **request_data**, the time series data you post to the API point.

It returns the API call response in JSON data."

(Detector 2023)

Keep in mind the following design principles when you put in place your API:

You should understand each sensor information connected to the AI.

It would help if you had the sensor data patterns that will trigger an Anomaly.

You should have a physical Alarm System for acute emergencies if the application is critical.

When you train the AI, you should work with the Manufacturing Team to get the following information:

Clean data

The AI must detect Test Scenarios that are critical for the System.

Although the AI can learn alone, the parameters used to get the Detection of the Anomaly must be documented and verified by the Technical Department.

In the case of Preventive Maintenance, there is information from companies that implemented Anomalies Detection in their Systems with hardware sensors and triggers.

QR III

PART IV

Omar Silva-Fulchi   AI   <u>info@robo-geek.ca</u>

Chapter X

Generative AI

"Generative AI is an artificial intelligence that uses unsupervised learning algorithms to create new digital content based on existing content, such as images, video, audio, text, or code. One of the most promising advances in AI, generative AI can learn the underlying pattern related to the input and generate plausible and creative content without human biases. A common technique for generative AI is generative adversarial networks (GANs), which use two neural networks, a generator, and a discriminator, that compete to produce and evaluate the new content." **(B.-C. Microsoft 2023)**

The following figure shows a block diagram of a GAN network made by Microsoft Edge AI.

The center box is the discriminator, a classifier that distinguishes accurate data from an original image with fake data created by a generator. The center of the box is the new content.

The discriminator has the left input for the fake data and the right input for the accurate data on each square side. The top right corner is the bank of authentic images, and the bottom left corner contains the fake pictures generated.

129

ChatGPT

ChatGPT is a member of the generative pre-trained transformer (GPT) family of language models. **(Wikipedia 2022)**

OpenAI team developed and released in November 2022 ChatGPT, an artificial intelligence (AI) chatbot.

US officials named a range of risks the public faces in the extensive adoption of AI tools, including the possible use of AI-created deep fakes and misinformation that could damage the democratic process. Job losses linked to increasing automation, biased algorithmic decision-making, physical dangers from autonomous vehicles, and the threat of AI-powered malicious hackers are on the US government's list of concerns. **(CNN 2023)**

Conversation with Microsoft Edge AI

Here you have a dialog with Microsoft Edge AI; there are slight changes in the answers of the Chat Bot AI to comply with grammar and syntax rules. I have also added references in the phrases used by the Chat Bot AI with a plagiarism checker.

Which AI module do you use?

I am a chatbot powered by Microsoft Bing search. I use a

combination of natural language processing, machine learning, and web search to understand and respond to user queries. I do not use a specific generative AI model, but I have access to tools such as graphic_art to generate content using generative AI models.

What is graphic_art?

Graphic_art is a tool that I have access to, which can generate graphical artwork using an artificial intelligence model. You can provide a prompt, and the tool will generate an image based on that prompt. if you give the prompt "a dragon," the tool will generate a picture of a dragon.

What other tools do you have access to?

In addition to graphic_art, I can access other tools that help me respond to user queries. For example, I can use search_web to search the web for information related to a user's query and provide a response based on the search results. I also have access to request_ads, which allows me to request advertisements relevant to the user's messages.

Please show me a graphical picture of Generative AI.

Sure, I'll try to create a graphical picture of Generative AI. Generative AI is an artificial intelligence that uses unsupervised learning algorithms to develop new digital content based on existing content, such as images, video, audio, text, or code. One of the most promising advances in AI, generative AI can learn the underlying pattern related to the input and generate plausible and creative content without human biases. A common technique for generative AI is generative adversarial networks (GANs), which use two neural networks, a generator, and a discriminator, competing to produce and evaluate the new content.

Here are two pictures of Generative AI created by Microsoft Bing Image Creator powered by DALL-E.

IMAGE 1: "GENERATIVE AI" Created by Microsoft Bing Image Creator powered by DALL-E.

IMAGE 2: "GENERATIVE AI" Created by Microsoft
Bing Image Creator powered by DALL-E.

How will GAI affect the economy and Jobs?

In the following link, you can find a complete report
of the article "The Potentially Large Effects of Artificial

Intelligence on Economic Growth." (Bridggs/Kodnani) on the Goldman Sachs (GS) site.

(Briggs/Kodnani 2023)

GS team analyzes how Generative AI could impact Economic Growth, Jobs, and Productivity in the next decade.

Joseph Briggs and Devesh Kodnani identified how the business adoption of Generative Artificial Intelligence (**GAI**) in production, services, automation, healthcare, and others could make significant growth changes in those areas.

Here are three projections they explained in their report:

- GAI could raise annual US labor productivity growth by, on average, 1.5 pp (percentage points) over ten years by adapting extensive business processes.

- GAI could increase annual global GDP by 7% over ten years, almost a **$7 trillion** increase in annual global GDP.

- Generative AI will be disruptive to jobs. Almost 60% of current jobs could implement AI automation, and the GAI could substitute up to 25% of current jobs.

How to deal with AI and ChatGPT?

In the last months I have read posts, articles, and interviews about Artificial Intelligence and GAI. Some statistics are precise, but other conclusions are out of context.

Effectively discoveries will affect our economies and jobs; however, we should be aware that we, as men, are the creation of God with unlimited possibilities.

When we are young, we have all dreams and are not afraid of failures or disappointments.

Technology has grown immensely in the last 50 years; we have adapted to the Internet, e-mail, the Cloud, and, lately, intelligent phones that carry our lives there.

It is important to remember that technology is a tool that should be used to enhance our lives and not replace them.

The most important is to learn about the careers we love at school, college, or university; if we work on what we love, our lives are fulfilled.

Regulating AI and GAIs at the government level is essential to optimize their usage and manage the percentage of jobs AI can take.

How to use Microsoft Edge AI?

Go to your PC or laptop and open Microsoft Edge, look for something you want to know about. I am writing ChatGPT.

The browser will open, then go to the Chat Tab.

Go to the Chat Tab and chat with Edge AI; this interface is better for discovering different topics. You stay in the same interface, and Edge AI gives you links to learn more about its findings.

If you master a topic, be prepared although the AI has much information about it, it may not know all. The AI needs to be smarter to make decisions with the data with human supervision and criteria.

From the chat you can ask Microsoft Edge AI to generate an image

BARD

Google invented the 2017 LAMDA (Language Model for Dialogue Applications). LAMBDA is a conversational AI model capable of fluid dialogue. In May 2023, Google made Bard available in 180 countries.

Currently, Bard supports Japanese, Korean, and US English.

We could not evaluate it because Google has yet to release Bard in Canada.

GLOBAL AI REGULATIONS

There are many proposals to regulate AI in different countries since 2020.

"The European Commission Published a legislative proposal for an "Artificial Intelligence Act "(AI Act) in April 2021" **(Congress 2021)**

The USA Senate and House introduced "The Algorithmic Accountability Act in February 2022.

In June 2022, the Canadian federal government introduced Bill C-27, the "Digital Charter Implementation Act", which contains newly proposed legislation relating to consumer privacy, data protection, and the first comprehensive laws governing artificial intelligence (AI) systems in Canada.

Here is an analysis from Japan-CSIS about AI Governance before G7 summit: **(CSIS 2023)**

"Japan's Leadership toward International Collaboration on AI Governance DIFFERENCES AND COMMONALITIES AMONG G7 COUNTRIES As mentioned in the introduction, AI regulation is one of the most challenging topics for G7 leaders. So far, the approach of G7 countries seems to be categorized into two groups. The first group is trying to take a "holistic and hard-law-based" system, which sets forth obligations— such as governance, transparency, and security for at least high-risk AI—with

140

significant sanctions in case of violation (Category 1). France,

Germany, and Italy, where the EU AI Act would be applied, can be categorized into this group. Canada, which is proposing AIDA, is also included in this category. The second group takes a "sector-specific and soft-law-based" approach, which seeks to promote appropriate AI governance through nonbinding guidance (rather than through comprehensive AI regulation) while requiring transparency and data protection in some sectors (Category 2). Japan and the United Kingdom fall into this category. The United States is also in this group but may come closer to Category 1 if the Algorithmic Accountability Act or a similar bill is adopted in Congress."

OpenAI released ChatGPT™-4 on March 14, 2023. GPT™-4 solves complex problems accurately and is creative. Moreover, it can compose songs and write screenplays. Additionally, it passed the SAT and Uniform Bar Exams with top percentiles.

This event created concern about how this new tool will affect our daily life, the economy, and jobs.

On May 04, 2023, VP Kamala Harris met with the heads of Google, Microsoft, Antrophic, and OpenAI to discuss the risks in the development of AI.

The G7 summit was in Hiroshima, Japan in May 19-21, 2023. **(White 2023)**

141

On May 20, 2023, the G7 countries have committed to further advancing multi-stakeholder approaches to developing standards for AI, respecting legally binding frameworks, and recognizing the importance of procedures that increase transparency, openness, fair processes, impartiality, privacy, and inclusiveness to promote responsible AI. They also stress the importance of international discussions on AI governance and interoperability between AI governance frameworks.

On June 14, 2023, EU lawmakers passed "The EU AI Act. "This is the first comprehensive set of regulations for the artificial intelligence industry." **(CNBC-Tech 2023)**

The law proposes requiring review Generative AI systems, such as ChatGPT, before commercial release. It also seeks to ban real-time facial recognition.

It occurs as worldwide regulators are racing to get a handle on the AI technology and moderate the risks to society, including job security and politics.

QR IV

Omar Silva-Fulchi   AI   <u>info@robo-geek.ca</u>

BIBLIOGRAPHY

Agent, Microsoft- Power Virtual. 2023. *Add Power Virtual Agents chatbot - Teams | Microsoft Learn.* 06 13. Accessed 07 07, 2023. https://learn.microsoft.com/en-us/microsoftteams/platform/bots/how-to/add-power-virtual-agents-bot-to-teams.

Anomaly-Detection, Microsoft-. 2022. *Anomaly Detector API Documentation.* 11 11. Accessed 07 05, 2023. https://learn.microsoft.com/en-us/azure/cognitive-services/anomaly-detector/.

Briggs/Kodnani. 2023. *Goldman Sachs: The Potentially Large Effects of Artificial Intelligence on Economic Growth.* 03 26. Accessed 06 14, 2023. https://www.gspublishing.com/content/research/en/reports/2023/03/27/d64e052b-0f6e-45d7-967b-d7be35fabd16.html.

Britannica. 2023. *3D manufacturing.* 3 8. Accessed 05 25, 2023. https://www.britannica.com/technology/3D-printing.

CNBC-Tech. 2023. *EU lawmakers pass landmark artificial intelligence regulation.* 06 14. Accessed 06 27, 2023. https://www.cnbc.com/2023/06/14/eu-lawmakers-pass-landmark-artificial-intelligence-regulation.html.

CNN. 2023. *Biden administration unveils an AI plan ahead of meeting with tech CEOs.* 05 05. Accessed 05 06, 2023. https://www.cnn.com/2023/05/04/tech/white-house-ai-plan.

Congress, Library of. 2021. *European Union: Commission Publishes Proposal to Regulate Artificial Intelligence.* 05 26. Accessed 06 27,

2023. https://www.loc.gov/item/global-legal-monitor/2021-05-26/european-union-commission-publishes-proposal-to-regulate-artificial-intelligence/.

Coop, Robo-Geek -Varun and Azaan. 2021. *Rock Paper Scissors Project for Robo-Geek.* August 3. Accessed 07 03, 2023. https://drive.google.com/file/d/1u6Y35YWjAMy-PUhAk8t6eeRIXjpSyAuF/view?usp=sharing.

CSIS, AI Regulation. 2023. *Japan's Approach to AI Regulation and Its Impact on the 2023 G7 Presidency.* 02 14. Accessed 06 25, 2023. https://www.csis.org/analysis/japans-approach-ai-regulation-and-its-impact-2023-g7-presidency.

Decisions, Tech. 2021. *IBM, Siemens Bring The Hybrid Cloud To Industrial IoT.* 3 2. Accessed 5 23, 2023. https://mytechdecisions.com/it-infrastructure/ibm-siemens-bring-the-hybrid-cloud-to-industrial-iot/.

Detector, Microsoft- Azure Anomaly. 2023. *Introducing Azure Anomaly Detector API - Microsoft Community Hub.* 05 11. Accessed 07 05, 2023. https://techcommunity.microsoft.com/t5/ai-customer-engineering-team/introducing-azure-anomaly-detector-api/ba-p/490162.

Google. 2023. 02 06. Accessed 02 06, 2023. https://ai.google/static/documents/ai-principles-2022-progress-update.pdf.

Google, Big Query. 2022. *Supply Chain Twin: Demo.* 07 07. Accessed 05 18, 2023. https://www.youtube.com/watch?v=r89RAjZkwLw.

146

I/O'19, Google- Tensorflow at. 2019. *Machine Learning Zero to Hero.* 05 05. Accessed 06 27, 2019. https://www.youtube.com/watch?v=VwVg9jCtqaU.

IBM. 2019. *What are digital twins?* November 14. Accessed February 6, 2023. https://developer.ibm.com/articles/what-are-digital-twins/.

IBM, Rest API. 2020. *What is a REST API?* 11 20. Accessed 07 08, 2023. https://www.ibm.com/topics/rest-apis.

IoT, Microsoft - Learn -. 2022. *Model and track the International Space Station with Azure Digital Twins and Data Explorer.* 4 7. Accessed 06 16, 2023. https://learn.microsoft.com/en-us/shows/internet-of-things-show/model-and-track-the-international-space-station-with-azure-digital-twins-and-data-explorer.

Kodnani), Goldman Sachs (Briggs /. 2023. *The Potentially Large Effects of Artificial Intelligence on Economic.* 3 26. Accessed 6 14, 2023. The Potentially Large Effects of Artificial Intelligence on Economic Growth (Briggs/Kodnani) (gspublishing.com).

—. 2023. *The Potentially Large Effects of Artificial Intelligence on Economic Growth.* 3 2023. Accessed 06 14, 2023. The Potentially Large Effects of Artificial Intelligence on Economic Growth (Briggs/Kodnani) (gspublishing.com).

Microsoft. 2022. *Develop secure embedded applications with Azure RTOS.* 11 29. Accessed 05 23, 2023. https://learn.microsoft.com/en-us/azure/iot-develop/concepts-azure-rtos-security-practices.

147

—. 2023. *How Microsoft drives responsible AI.* January 27. Accessed January 27, 2023. https://www.microsoft.com/en-us/ai/our-approach?activetab=pivot1%3aprimaryr5.

—. 2021. *Microsoft-Azure Digital Twins.* February 12. Accessed 05 17, 2023. https://azure.microsoft.com/en-ca/products/digital-twins/.

—. 2022. *Responsible AI.* June. Accessed 02 04, 2023. https://blogs.microsoft.com/wp-content/uploads/prod/sites/5/2022/06/Microsoft-RAI-Impact-Assessment-Guide.pdf.

Microsoft, - Power Virtual Agent. 2020. *Virtual Agents within Microsoft Teams.* 9 22. Accessed 07 07, 2023. https://powervirtualagents.microsoft.com/en-us/blog/announcing-public-preview-of-power-virtual-agents-within-microsoft-teams/.

Microsoft, Bing-Chat. 2023. *What is Generative AI?* Richmond Hill, 05 05.

Microsoft, Chatbots in Microsoft Teams. 2021. *Chatbots in Microsoft Teams | Build with Power Virtual Agents.* 07 06. Accessed 07 05, 2023. https://www.youtube.com/watch?v=G8C_YKdJves.

Microsoft, Power Virtual Agents Documentation. 2022. *Microsoft Power Virtual Agents documentation.* 05 03. Accessed 07 03, 2023. https://learn.microsoft.com/en-us/power-virtual-agents/.

Microsoft, Rest API reference. 2023. *Azure REST API reference.* 04 03. Accessed 07 08, 2023. https://learn.microsoft.com/en-us/rest/api/azure/.

Moroney, Laurence. 2018. *Rock Paper Scissors (using Convolutional Neural Network).* 05 18. Accessed 01 15, 2019. https://colab.research.google.com/drive/1cndJp-5g-p-yP61K4Flx9MR3HR_OBH1D?usp=sharing.

NASA. 2023. *International Space Station -Expedition 69,ISS.* 06 15. Accessed 06 29, 2023. https://www.nasa.gov/image-feature/view-of-the-international-space-station-during-a-spacewalk.

Robo-Geek. 2023. *Colab first program.* 06 21. Accessed 06 21, 2023. https://colab.research.google.com/drive/1PKNpBKIqOt Q1xx7_Hhk0uWLXo49EBbbm?usp=sharing.

Robo-Geek-CNN. 2019. *Project Rock Paper Scissors using CNN at Robo-Geek.* 06 27. Accessed 07 28, 2019. https://colab.research.google.com/drive/1cndJp-5g-p-yP61K4Flx9MR3HR_OBH1D?usp=sharing.

SIEMENS Team, SOFTWARE PLM. 2019. *SIEMENS Closed-loop manufacturing White Paper.* April 18. Accessed 04 28, 2023. https://resources.sw.siemens.com/en-US/white-paper-closed-loop-manufacturing.

Silva-Zapata, Omar. 2019. *Manufacturing Workshop.* February 02. Accessed 04 27, 2023. https://drive.google.com/file/d/1RbJ-yroEZIQTfRUsKzqrmMiZzDgs9vMQ/view?usp=sharing.

—. 2018. *RG-680 - ML.* 04 15. Accessed 03 16, 2019. https://drive.google.com/file/d/1oDfgEGgUCOQ98-y7dMpidqwOlnLQx1w7/view?usp=sharing.

—. 2016. *STEM Neural Networks*. 05 12. Accessed 06 18, 2020. https://drive.google.com/file/d/14hLQbxhRaIY96YJccxf HD-MfhHvlRZVJ/view?usp=sharing.

Telecom.com. 2023. *Samsung, IBM partner to combine "edge computing" with private 5G networks*. 3 6. Accessed 5 23, 2023. https://telecom.economictimes.indiatimes.com/news/sam sung-ibm-partner-to-combine-edge-computing-with-private-5g-networks/79770677.

-TPU, Google. 2017. *Build and train machine learning models on our new Google Cloud TPUs*. 03 17. Accessed 06 21, 2023. https://blog.google/products/google-cloud/google-cloud-offer-tpus-machine-learning/.

White, House. 2023. *G7 Hiroshima Leaders' Communiqué*. 05 20. Accessed 07 07, 2023. https://www.whitehouse.gov/briefing-room/statements-releases/2023/05/20/g7-hiroshima-leaders-communique/.

Wikipedia. 2022. *ChatGPT*. Dec 8. Accessed 05 05, 2023. https://en.wikipedia.org/wiki/ChatGPT.

Omar Silva-Fulchi   AI   <u>info@robo-geek.ca</u>

ACKNOWLEDGES

Ali Juma

Omar Silva Zapata

Karen Wonders

Elizabeth Wong

MEV Innovation Centre

PEO – York Chapter

PMI- Toronto Chapter

Promoción 28 del Colegio Claretiano

SME (Society of Manufacturing Engineering)

St. Francis Xavier Catholic Secondary School

    Ms. Holly Roberts

    Varun Joshi

    Azaan Kamran

    Syed Musab Saqib

UNI-CC-El Computito

UNICC-Tigrillos

    Oscar Adaniya

    Oscar Cabanillas

    Jorge Martinez

    Julio Porcel

    Carlos Villacrez

    Manuel Yrigoyen

UNI-69

    David Caceres

    Fernando Campos Merino

    Ciro Sotomayor

    Práxedes Espejo

    Medardo Garcia-Paico

    Gustavo Hung

    Coco Lavalle

Hugo Meza

Lucho Geldres

Luis Horna Diaz

Denny Landaveri

James Bravo

Manuel Marquez

Manuel Velasquez

Luis Villanueva

Omar Silva-Fulchi   AI   <u>info@robo-geek.ca</u>

Omar Silva-Fulchi   AI   info@robo-geek.ca

Omar Silva-Fulchi   AI   <u>info@robo-geek.ca</u>